*Juneau
Portrait II*

Juneau Portrait II

PHOTOS BY *Mark Kelley*

ESSAYS BY ANNABEL LUND

I would like to dedicate this book to my parents, Dan and Betty Lou Kelley, who gave me their love, my education and my first camera even though times were tough.

This book would not have been published without the hard work of Odette Foster, Larry Persily, Linda Daniel and Annabel Lund.
Thanks to Laura Lucas for making the book look so beautiful.
Thanks to all who interviewed with Annabel, including: Bob Banghart, Elsa Demeksa, Titti Gallizio, Clark Gruening, Dennis Harris, T. Terry Harvey, Nancy Waterman, Hilary Lindh, Cliff Lobaugh, Rie Munoz, Marie Olson, John Palmes, Larry Parker, Ernie Polley, Rudy Ripley, Caren Robinson, Linda Rosenthal and Dr. Walter Soboleff.
Thanks to all who helped us find historic memorabilia including: Jeff Brown, Joan Cahill, Scott Foster, Chris Garrison, Skip Gray, Donna Hatton, Bob Janes, Sandro Lane, Marcie and Geoff Larson, Carol McCabe, Dan Owen and Jerry Shriner.
Thanks to the Alaska State Library and the Juneau-Douglas City Museum for their assistance with historic photos and artifacts and for their dedication to preserving Juneau's history.
Thanks to Connie DePute and the staff at Hearthside Books for telling me it was time to do another book on Juneau.
Thanks to the *Juneau Empire* and Mr. William Morris III. Without their understanding over the years, many of these photos would not exist.
Thanks to Juneauites for making Juneau such a wonderful place to photograph.
Special thanks goes to my wife, Jan, and our two sons, Gabe and Owen whose love and support I cherish.

Half-title page photo: Auke Lake and the Mendenhall Glacier
Title page photo: North Douglas, Alaska

Publisher, Photographer, Project Editor: Mark Kelley
Cover and Book Design: Laura Lucas
Writers: Annabel Lund and Linda Daniel
Text Editor: Larry Persily
Researcher and Proofreader: Odette Foster
Proofreaders: Mary Bowen, Paula Cadiente and Rick Keifer

To order single copies of *Juneau Portrait II*, mail $29.95 each for a hardcover edition or $19.95 each for a softbound edition plus $5.00 for shipping to Mark Kelley, P.O. Box 20470, Juneau, AK 99802.
Booksellers: Retail discounts are available from Mark Kelley, P.O. Box 20470, Juneau, Alaska, 99802.
Toll-free: 1-888-933-1993; Phone: 907-586-1993; E-mail: photos@markkelley.com; Web page: www.markkelley.com

Printed in Korea
First printing, March 1997
Second printing, January 1998
Third printing, December 2000
Fourth printing, December 2002

ISBN I-880865-08-4 (hardcover)
ISBN I-880865-09-2 (softcover)
Library of Congress Catalog Card Number: 96-94897

─ Rainbow over Downtown Juneau ─

~Auke Lake~

-THUNDER MOUNTAIN-

I was a college student in my 20s when I visited Juneau for the first time — and I've had a crush on the town ever since. I came down from the University of Alaska Fairbanks for a week-long course on the state government. It was April 1977, and the sun was out the entire week. More than two years passed before I could get back.

Even after I moved here, it took a few more years before I knew this romance would last. On a late-March day in the early 1980s, it snowed overnight in the mountains and the day dawned clear blue and snowflake-clean. I caught the first chair at Eaglecrest and skied a half-dozen runs before rushing downtown to board a sailboat in order to photograph the season's opening race. As the last boat crossed the finish line, I headed back to Eaglecrest to get in a few more runs before last chair. That evening I went out to eat, and after dinner I walked out — and into a stunning display of northern lights. I thought to myself "only in Juneau," and from that day forward I knew Juneau was home.

In 1982, I published *Juneau Portrait*, a black-and-white photo book and my first publishing venture. I'm now in my 40s, the college days are long gone, and life has been good. I'm married with two sons, a house, a downtown office and two four-wheel-drive station wagons — and *Juneau Portrait II* is a reality. This collection of color photos shows you some of my favorites. Usually, a portrait is taken in flattering light when the subject is looking their best. This portrait of Juneau is no different. The light is flattering, the place is looking great and the sun is out. It is these stunningly sunny days that keep me addicted to Juneau and photography.

I hope you enjoy the photos in this book as much as I loved shooting them in this remarkable place.

Mark Kelley

AUGUST 1996

← *Northern lights*

9

*J*uneau is enormous yet tiny. The city limits encompass 3,248 square miles, twice the size of Rhode Island. And yet fewer than 30,000 souls make their homes here.

Our town is more park than city. Greater than 90 percent is covered by coastline, forest, mountains and ice fields, all nestled within the largest national forest in the nation. The community rejects skyscrapers, preferring scenic vistas of mountain peaks. Summits 3,500 feet high ring downtown Juneau. On the nearby Juneau Icefield, the Mendenhall Towers scrape the sky at nearly 7,000 feet. The paved road system stretches north only about 38 miles, while hiking trails measure more than 130 miles.

Whatever the distance, recreational opportunities abound. In the spring and summer there is hiking, fishing, camping and boating. The U.S. Coast Guard counts 3,850 vessels registered in Juneau, most used for recreation. Intramural sports for adults and youngsters fill Juneau's 20 ballparks year-round. Football, ice hockey and cross-country skiing replace softball, soccer and Rollerblading as the seasons change.

In the winter, the kayaks and bicycles strapped to car roofs are replaced by snowboards and downhill and cross-country skis. Municipally owned Eaglecrest, one of the few ski areas in the world on an island, is as challenging as it is beautiful. Eaglecrest is proud of the ski champions it produces, including the downhill silver medal winner of the 1992 Olympics, Hilary Lindh, and several of the top competitors in the Junior Olympics.

A significant portion of the population fishes in the summer and hunts in the autumn, filling freezers with the abundant wildlife resources inhabiting the rich waters and fertile forests nearby. A Juneau family may supplement its annual food budget with venison, salmon, halibut, fresh fowl and plump berries.

In no other capital city in America will you find bears sauntering past the state courthouse, mountain goats teetering above your jogging path or bald eagles

⌐ Cross country skier enjoys solitude at Spaulding Meadows.

"As the capital city, we attract professionals in all areas, people to whom life without music, theater or art is unimaginable." LINDA ROSENTHAL

shorting out power lines. It is thrilling to observe humpback whales, sea lions, black-tailed deer and great blue herons, all without leaving the city limits.

Even after 26 years in Juneau, Nancy Waterman is still charmed to see bear and deer graze outside the door of her downtown home. "The other day we took a canoe out to Cohen Island and just kind of floated along in the water watching a couple of whales coming and going all around us," Waterman says. "Those are the things you never get tired of. Those are the things that keep you here."

When *Outside Magazine* rated Juneau fifth on its list of America's Most Livable Communities in 1993, its writer observed, "There is a snap in the air in Juneau, a guiding intelligence. I've never run into a more eclectic, smart, politically and culturally aware populace in a town so small."

Boasting sophistication typically found in larger cities, Juneau supports a symphony orchestra, a university, a lyric opera company and two professional theaters. Art galleries and fine restaurants outnumber gas stations. Three news-papers, seven radio and television stations and five libraries thrive.

In 1986, classical musician Linda Rosenthal helped establish the Juneau Jazz & Classics Festival, which continues to draw top-name artists. Some of the most popular performances are held aboard cruises of nearby waters — blues and classical concerts with backdrops of stunning seascapes.

She says the community's prosperity translates "into a cultural broadness and openness, a high degree of sophistication. As the capital city, we attract professionals in all areas, people to whom life without music, theater or art is unimaginable."

Since 1974, folk musicians have invaded town for the week-long Alaska Folk Festival, with thousands attending the concerts and workshops put on by dozens of performers. Attendance is free to music lovers throughout the Pacific Northwest who herald the coming of spring by traveling to Juneau each April for the festivities.

⌐ Above: *Buzz Ritter and John Lager warm up at Lager's downtown shoe shop for the Alaska Folk Festival.*
⌐ Opposite page: *Violinist Linda Rosenthal plays at the University of Alaska Southeast campus at Auke Lake.*

Celebration '96 participants parade through downtown.

Every two years Native dance troupes from Alaska and Canada arrive in Juneau to celebrate Native music and dance. Celebration '96 included 40 troupes and more than 1,000 performers. This celebration of Native tradition and ceremony is also a spiritual assembly, uniting people of common heritage and commitment to their culture.

"The Western impact on the Tlingit people was such that the Native traditional singing and dancing and various ceremonials were put away. The Tlingit people, in appreciation of their traditions, felt they should bring them out again. You might call it a revival, a cultural renaissance," says Walter Soboleff, a Tlingit who served a Presbyterian congregation in Juneau for more than 20 years. He later acted as department head of Native Studies at the University of Alaska Fairbanks from 1970 to 1974 and chairman of the Board of Trustees for Sealaska Heritage Foundation in Juneau.

For many of the tiny villages scattered along the Alaska Panhandle, however, the most important annual celebration hosted by Juneau is the Lions Club Gold Medal Basketball Tournament. Dozens of teams battle it out at the high school gym, their competitive instincts sharpened by 50 years of determined yet good-natured sports rivalries. Cheering in the bleachers are families and friends for whom Gold Medal is more than a sporting event. It is a week of reuniting with old friends, strengthening alliances formed generations ago.

All of this helps Juneau retain the best of a small-town soul. Many people still think nothing of leaving their doors unlocked; strangers collect helpful tips, not suspicious glances. It's telling that Juneau police feel it necessary to make public announcements urging residents not to leave their keys in their cars' ignitions.

"I can let my sons play outside or visit friends without giving a thought to their safety," says Juneau businesswoman Elsa Demeksa. "They can be outside for hours in the woods or the backyard and you know they're all right. Sometimes I watch my son walk off to school and I realize how safe he is. And I say to myself, 'Thank you, Lord'."

Demeksa was born in Ethiopia and schooled in Europe and the East Coast. Her father, a diplomat and international banker, spoke eloquently of his 1972 visit to

Alaska, urging his daughter to see it for herself. "Of course, the first day I got here I knew I'd never leave. I fell in love with it. I got off the ferry at 2 a.m. and the northern lights were out like a welcoming sign, a message from above. My father was furious. He would say, 'I told you to visit. I never told you to stay there!'" Demeksa laughs.

Still, there are some animosities, albeit friendly ones. Douglas has never quite forgiven Juneau for usurping its position as the center of town, even though that encroachment took place more than a century ago. Cars on the west side of the bridge have been known to sport bumper stickers that boast "Douglas: The Gateway to Juneau," and for several years Douglas passports were available at the neighborhood grocery.

On the Fourth of July, Douglas asserts its independence and reminisces about its pre-bridge glory days when it was larger and more sophisticated than Juneau by sponsoring its own Fourth of July parade with its own parade marshals. The fact that the Douglas parade includes essentially the same tissue-papered floats, Boy Scout color guard and bagpipe marching band as the Juneau parade two hours earlier takes nothing away from the enthusiasm.

Douglas may have started as a mining town but Juneau belonged to Tlingits for hundreds of years. Walter Soboleff was a young child when he first accompanied his Angoon family to Juneau for a 1912 shopping trip.

"Juneau was the summer subsistence area for the Aak' w Kwann Clan. They came for the summers because the creeks had fish. The men would go up the canyons and mountains for goats, and the women would pick berries.

"I used to hear stories about this mountain back of Juneau (Mount Juneau). Its Tlingit name means 'Glowing Mountain.' On clear nights when the moon is shining, it almost appears as if it's glowing; the reflection off the ice field probably."

Shriners in the Fourth of July parade drive up South Franklin.

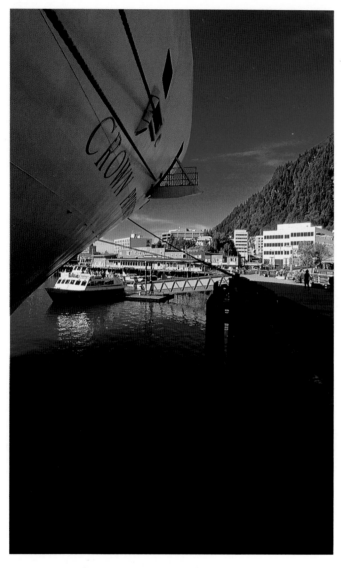

Above: Cruise ship docks at downtown Juneau.

Opposite page: The evening light brings to a close a wintery day in downtown Juneau.

The Tlingits, and their influence on Juneau, remain vigorous, vocal and dignified. There is also a powerful and dynamic Filipino community in Juneau. Many were originally lured to Alaska by jobs in the fish processing industry but stayed to open other businesses, raise their families and participate in community life.

All cultures understand that laughter is good for what ails us, and Juneau respects a well-developed sense of humor, frequently applying a dose of tranquilizing satire to our aches and pains.

James Watt, the controversial, pro-development Secretary of the Interior under President Ronald Reagan, says the most creative demonstration he saw was in Juneau: a 21-chain saw salute on the steps of the Capitol, lined with environmentalists dressed as Sitka spruce.

Juneau also nurtures humor's first cousin, whimsy. At the Save the Raisins Party, elegant, formally clad townsfolk gathered atop Mount Juneau to waltz the summer evening away, accompanied by a baby grand piano airlifted to the peak for the occasion.

The same qualities that make Juneau a wonderful place to live make Juneau a wonderful place to visit. Breathtaking scenery, fascinating history, friendly people, cultural events and accessible wilderness attract half a million tourists each year.

Juneau is the cruise ship capital of Alaska. With as many as 400 ship landings each season, it is common on a summer day to find tourists outnumbering residents on downtown streets. The cruise ship industry rates Southeast Alaska second only to the Caribbean in market appeal, and a recent poll of passengers rated Juneau the fifth most popular vacation destination in the world.

For all of Juneau's charm, the weather, isolation and high cost of living means sacrifice. A typical winter brings 100 inches of snow. Some soggy years, the warmth of the sun can feel hemispheres away. "There is some good to all of that rain," says Juneau artist Rie Munoz. "The reason I get so much artwork done is directly related to Juneau's annual rainfall. When it rains, I paint."

"I used to hear stories about this mountain back of Juneau. Its Tlingit name means 'Glowing Mountain.' On clear nights when the moon is shining, it almost appears as if it's glowing; the reflection off the ice field probably." DR. WALTER SOBOLEFF

"There is some good to all of that rain. The reason I get so much artwork done is directly related to Juneau's annual rainfall. When it rains, I paint." RIE MUÑOZ

⌐ *Rie Munoz poses for a portrait in her gallery in the Mendenhall Valley.*

There are no roads to Juneau, which is accessible only by boat or plane. Air travel is a necessity here, and the high cost of transportation translates into a higher cost of living. Everything from apples to shoelaces, building supplies to bandages must be barged or flown into town.

Maybe it forces people to appreciate more of what they have. "Juneau has an appealing contrast of urban stimulation surrounded by unexcelled natural beauty and tranquility," says Clark Gruening, grandson of the late Territorial Governor Ernest Gruening.

Restaurateur T. Terry Harvey says Juneau's many contrasts provide a little bit of everything for everybody. "What makes Juneau really work is the balance of the mix," he says. "For every lawyer or bureaucrat you throw into the stew, there's a biker or a cook or a fisherman. But no matter how diverse we are, we still have to sit on the same bench at the swimming pool sauna."

Juneau is a prosperous town. Although we fall prey to the same boom-and-bust economic forces that have always shaped the resource-rich Last Frontier, Juneau has suffered less during lean times. The misery of the Great Depression was made more bearable by mining company paychecks; when those ran out during World War II, government payrolls took over.

Today more than half of the working populace receives paychecks from federal, state, municipal and Native corporation offices. The average family income is about $54,000; the average unemployment rate is 5 percent.

Like other capitals, this is an unabashedly partisan town that takes its democracy seriously. The life of the city revolves around government and the 121-day annual legislative session. Each winter, the streets are swollen with support staff and lobbyists sired by the presence of the state's 60 lawmakers. Although elections may mean new faces every few years, there is a comforting continuity in the process itself.

Alaskans enjoy a good-natured familiarity with their elected officials; most are on a first-name basis. No place is this more true than in Juneau where the lieutenant governor may stand shoulder-to-shoulder with constituents in the grocery checkout line, a crimson-faced, sweat-suited governor can be seen jogging up and down the narrow hilly streets, and the Speaker of the House sings in a church choir.

Governors of other states are typically—and of necessity —insulated from their neighbors by security guards. Not so here, where it is a point of pride that the state's highest executive may field an occasional voter complaint while sipping coffee at the counter of a downtown diner and the doorbell at his house may be answered by a smiling first lady.

"Only in Alaska! is a phrase we use a lot of here," says Juneau Representative Caren Robinson. She was an escapee from an abusive marriage when she moved to Juneau with her young son in May 1976.

"When I first got here, every day after work I'd walk through the rain to take (my son) Shane to the child-care center and we kept running into this same man all the time, coming and going. We'd say 'Hi!' talk about the weather, and go on," Robinson remembers. "One day we both happened to be walking in the same direction and when we got to the Governor's Mansion, he waved and said 'Bye!' and walked inside. I realized he was Governor (Jay) Hammond. Where else in the world do you find that?"

It is clear to Juneau residents the Governor's Mansion belongs to the people, not the politicians. A regular stop for trick-or-treaters on Halloween and clusters of Brownies hawking Girl Scout Thin Mints, the mansion's holiday open house marks the beginning of each Christmas season. In what other state capital is the entire population invited to sample eggnog and extravagant hors d'oeuvres with top officials, wander through the governor's home to ooh and ah over decorations, and sing traditional carols around a tree bristling with homemade ornaments?

Christmas lights brighten the Governor's Mansion.

"*Stay here long enough and you will lose your ability to distinguish between self and place. That is what Juneau is all about.*"   ERNIE POLLEY

— Berners Bay sunset

"Speaking of the constants which define Juneau: Mount Juneau in midwinter during a full moon; the smell of saltwater; the Fourth of July fireworks," former mayor Ernie Polley says, adding to his list. "The words '10- to 20-knot southeasterlies with intermittent rain' as the most familiar words in the weather forecast; the comfort of the all-purpose footwear, the rubber boot."

The images are not reserved only for old-timers. World travelers Titti Gallizio and her husband Giorgio are recent arrivals, having built their home in Juneau in 1992 and their restaurant in 1995. Titti Gallizio says she never wanted anything so badly in her life.

"Suddenly I knew this had to be my place. This had to be my home. I said, 'I can die here. I will die here. I don't need anything more.

"Why did I fall in love with this place? Magic, something that cannot be explained. I have never been happier in my life. When I am standing on a rock fishing, looking at the sea and the sky, I feel my spirit lifting. I am closer to God," she says.

"It is humbling. I see how small we are and how large are the mountains, the sea, the sky, and I know just beyond this mountain there is nothing, no people, no roads. It is a strange feeling, a humbling feeling. This is really something special, this town and the deep feelings of magic here. For me, at my age, it is like a dessert, a sweet, the cake at the end of my meal."

Just as it happened to Titti Gallizio, it happens to others. "If you stay long enough — and for some I suspect this happens the first day they are here — you will lose your ability to conceive of living anywhere else," Ernie Polley says. "Stay here long enough and you will lose your ability to distinguish between self and place. That is what Juneau is all about."

Annabel Lund
August 1996

A SENSE OF PLACE

*J*uneau beckons like a welcome mat before a ruggedly beautiful frontier. On a sliver of land along the edge of the continent, it nestles against the coast mountains and faces the sea. It is civilization surrounded by wilderness. Six blocks up from the heart of the city, streets turn into hiking trails. One block down, pavement ends at the waterfront.

━ Above: Trio of lupine catch the warm light of evening sun.
━ Right: Two hikers view the archipelago looking north from a peak on the north of Douglas Island.

~ Sawmill Creek, Berners Bay ~

"*It is humbling. I see how small we are and how large are the mountains, the sea, the sky, and I know just beyond this mountain there is nothing, no people, no roads. It is a strange feeling, a humbling feeling.*" TITTI GALLIZIO

—Sockeye salmon swim along Steep Creek at the Mendenhall Glacier Recreation Area.

Spring

Spring in Juneau means the return of light. As the Earth tilts toward the equinox, daylight lingers longer with each day and human spirits rise. In between patches of snow, the ground is greening up. There is softness in the air and a touch of warmth in the sun.

— *Left: Skunk cabbage*
— *Above: Sitka black-tailed deer*

~ PETERSON SALT CHUCK ~

Summer

Summer is measured in wildflowers. It begins with yellow dandelions, suddenly scattered everywhere. Next comes the blue of lupine along the roadsides, followed by daisies, chocolate lilies and shooting stars. Midsummer is marked by the hot pink of fireweed. The bloom begins low on a spike of tight buds, spreading upward. When the tip of fireweed flowers, summer ends.

— Left: Lupine and dandelions
— Above: Field of fireweed in front of Auke Lake and the Mendenhall Glacier

— *Above: Crow in mountain ash*

Autumn

Autumn happens fast. Yesterday you were in shirtsleeves and sneakers. Today, you are in a downpour that feels like a sluice gate has opened overhead. The last of the snowbirds leave town, and soon only the locals are left — crows, eagles, ravens and people in rubber boots. But between successive Southeast weather fronts are glowing days so clear and bright that every line appears etched.

~ Moose Lake ~

Winter

*I*t's snowing by November, sometimes piling up 7 feet. More typically, there is just enough to tease the town into hopes of spending Thanksgiving weekend on skis. Christmas lights brighten the darkness closing in at each end of day. By winter solstice, the sun doesn't rise until almost 9 a.m. and doesn't linger much past 3 p.m. Icy Taku winds topple trees and steal garbage cans. There are a few sunny, crystalline days, but most of the time it is snowing, raining or "snaining"—something in between.

⟵ Left: Auke Bay Harbor
⟵ Above: Mendenhall Bar, North Douglas

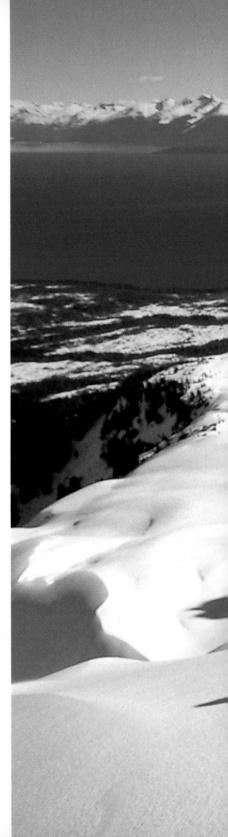

A Playground for all Seasons

Juneau loves to go out and play at any time of year. The choices range from simple to far out on the scale of adventure. On the athletic edge are parasailing, heli-skiing and climbing—your choice of mountain, rock or ice. River rafting and sea kayaking are popular with young and old alike. Walking in wild places is the universal sport, often combined with watching the wetland dabbling of migratory geese, picking wild blueberries for a pie, or beachcombing with the dog and kids. It is no wonder that Juneau consistently is named one of *Outside Magazine*'s top places to live.

Above: Rafters float the glacial-fed Mendenhall River.
Right: Helicopters provide access to the Chilkat Mountains for adventuresome skiers.

Skis, Skates and Snowboards

*W*inter sports range from cross-country skiing on bike paths to skating on lakes. Add an inclined slope, anything that slides —from sleds and saucers and inner tubes to snowboards —and you're catching air. Groomed slopes lure downhill skiers, and telemarkers head for the backcountry hills.

⌐ *Above: Hockey players on Auke Lake ice*
⌐ *Left: Skier at Eaglecrest in West Bowls*

-&- Eaglecrest Snowboarder -&-

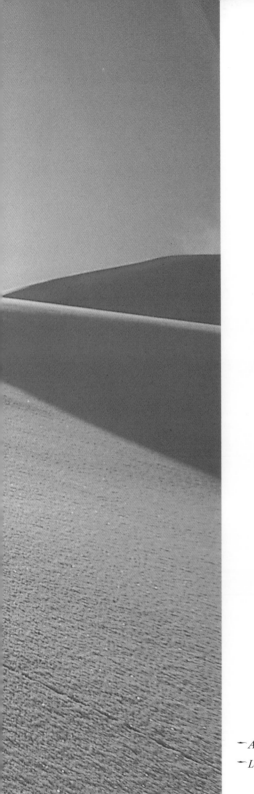

Eaglecrest—Rain or Shine

Some of the best ski slopes on the West Coast are just a 20-minute drive from downtown. The municipally owned ski area has two double-chair lifts. One is a half-mile long with a 600-foot drop. The other gives you a full mile ride uphill, then drops 1,400 feet. There also are two circuits of trails for skinny skis. No matter what the weather is doing at sea level, Eaglecrest is above it all. Youngsters greet a Saturday morning cold rain with whoops of delight, as it promises fresh powder on the mountain slopes. And when the weather up top is sloppy, Juneauites simply ski in rubberized rain gear.

Above: Ski to Sea relay race
Left: Eaglecrest skier

―*Above: Visitors enjoy glacial vista at the Mendenhall Visitor Center.*

The Glacial Phenomenon

*T*he Mendenhall Glacier is one of Alaska's top five attractions. In its home town, the backyard glacier is number one. It is the place one always offers to take the folks from out of town.

A glacier is a broad ribbon of ice flowing down from an ice field in mountains so high that snow remains year-round. Some snow may melt in the summer, but not enough to offset the amount that falls the rest of the year. As the snow accumulates, its weight causes it to compact, turning it into ice. It builds up until it overflows, pulled by gravity down valleys radiating from the great field of ice.

The Juneau Icefield is 1,500 square miles—larger than the state of Rhode Island and more than 30 glaciers flow from it. Big, beautiful Mendenhall Glacier is the most spectacular of them. Running 12 miles downhill, it is 1.5 miles wide at the face, where it cracks and showers icebergs into jewel-like Mendenhall Lake.

HELICOPTER TOUR, JUNEAU ICEFIELD

"Hanging out" at the Glacier

I t's hard to imagine a more scenic place than Mendenhall Lake, where the glacier's face provides a backdrop for skaters gliding across the ice. A nearby knob is alive with kids and sleds. Mountain bikers venture onto the ice, along with cross-country skiers—some under tow behind the family dog. Climbers practice their technique on huge icebergs caught fast in the frozen surface of the lake. In summer, the lakefront campground launches countless small craft to join a resident flock of sailboards.

Left: Parasailer catches the thermals above Thunder Mountain in the Mendenhall Valley.
Right: Ice climber rapels off the face of an iceberg frozen in Mendenhall Lake.

Fishing Fever

The first symptoms appear with the coming of Spring. Although the skiing is great, more and more people head for the harbor. They are the first wave in a series of seasonal migrations. Next come the spring king salmon, followed by early summer runs of pinks and chum. August brings coho, and then it is Golden North Salmon Derby time. Many shops traditionally close during derby days so employees, owners and customers can fish. When someone says "fishing" you assume they're talking about salmon, though it could be halibut so big you tow them to shore because they are too heavy to lift into your skiff or Dolly Varden caught from the shore at Eagle Beach.

— Jan Beauchamp with king salmon catch

—SNUG COVE, ADMIRALTY ISLAND—

Boats, Boats, Boats

*P*eople in Juneau love boats. Here, "learning to drive" does not necessarily mean wheels, and "Suzuki method" suggests starting them young on outboards, not violins. There are more boats in Juneau than anywhere else in Alaska except for Anchorage, which has 10 times as many residents. Juneau has 900 boats in slips at municipal harbors, 200 to 500 more in transient moorage, others at private moorings and about 3,000 more on trailers ready to roll to one of the many local boat launch ramps. It is unclear whether fishing provides a good excuse for a boat or if having a boat is a good excuse for fishing.

⌐Above: Nine-year-old Gabe Kelley, driving a skiff for the first time
⌐Right: Auke Bay with eclipsing moonset

Fishing on the Fly

As indicated by the guest logs in the U.S. Forest Service cabins on remote lakes, many fisherfolk fly in by floatplane to stay awhile in the Tongass National Forest wilderness. It is also common for fishing enthusiasts to fly in just long enough to catch a few nice cutthroat trout. Look in the cargo compartment of any floatplane moored at the airport pond or Auke Lake. Odds are you'll find a fishing rod.

Left: Sig Olson casts on Hasselborg Lake, Admiralty Island.

Above: Rich DiLorenzo fly fishes from float plane on Antler Lake.

Float Plane Fly Fishing on Antler Lake

WANDERLUST & WILDLIFE

*J*uneau neighbors—its emerald fiords—stir wanderlust. Carved by glaciers during the Ice Age, the labyrinth of islands and waterways is home to wildlife and wilderness that people come from around the world to see. Admiralty Island, Tracy Arm and Glacier Bay are the featured attractions. Admiralty, called by the Native people "Kootznoowoo" or the fortress of the bears, has the greatest density of brown bears in the world, one bear per square mile. The scenic beauty of the Tracy Arm-Ford's Terror Wilderness Area is as majestic today as when it moved the great naturalist, John Muir, to pen superlatives in his diary. Glacier Bay National Park is a symphony in ice.

Above: Harbor seal on iceberg at Glacier Bay National Park
Right: Wall of ice from tidewater Sawyer Glacier dwarfs the boat of an intrepid explorer in Tracy Arm.

"*The other day we took a canoe out to Cohen Island and just kind of floated along in the water watching a couple of whales coming and going all around us. Those are the things you never get tired of. Those are the things that keep you here.*"

NANCY WATERMAN

⌐ Above: Humpback whale sounds in front of a group of kayakers in Icy Strait.

⌐ Left: Kayaker paddles out of Amalga Harbor towards the Chilkat Mountains.

~Mountain Goats, Tracy Arm~

Tracy Arm

*J*ust 45 miles south of Juneau is Tracy Arm, a 25-mile long ribbon of water between steep cliffs, in most places, less than a mile wide.

From the sheltered waters of Holkham Bay, a favorite resting place for humpback whales, the narrow channel winds northward past a landscape that changes from the lush greenery to a world of ice. On the steep walls one can see the tracks of nature—the tilting and uplifting of the Earth's tectonic plates, the scars of glacial surges and retreats, the carving of bedrock by persistent streams and the softening influence of plant life.

On ice floes close to the faces of the Sawyer and South Sawyer Glaciers, seals haul out to give birth and nurse their pups. White dots that move on the mountainside are not patches of snow but mountain goats. Waterfalls tumble from neck-craning heights as bears meander the tide flats and red-legged pigeon guillemots line up side-by-side along crevices in the cliff.

Boat nudges up to a waterfall cascading down a steep cliff wall in Tracy Arm-Fords Terror Wilderness.

Humpback Whales

The life of the humpback whales seen feeding in the local waters are the envy of many people who live here. Most the humpbacks migrate each fall to the tropical waters of Mexico and Hawaii to sing, play and bear their young. Each spring, they return to Alaska to feed in the rich waters. A fascinating spectacle is the whales' bubble-net feeding. A group of humpbacks will submerge beneath a school of herring, then release bubbles that encircle the fish like a net. The whales then lunge from below, jaws agape making a clean sweep of the neatly gathered fish.

Above: Humpback whale breaches at sunset.
Left: Pod of humpbacks engage in bubble-net feeding.

Glacier Bay National Park

*I*t is the sheer expanse of Glacier Bay that visitors remember. Twelve tidewater glaciers advance and retreat, sculpting the landscape to define geologic time. Just 200 years ago, a wall of ice sealed the mouth of the bay. Now, spruce and hemlock shade a forest floor where moss softens every footfall and ferns and wildflowers abound. With each mile of travel into the bay, the landscape changes, revealing the succession of growth as plants colonize and then reclaim the ice-scoured rock. Wildlife varies with the habitat. Tufted puffins and horned puffins bob on the water, and kittiwakes wheel before the sheer rock walls where they nest. In Glacier Bay, geology becomes poetry.

Left: Face of Margerie Glacier at Glacier Bay National Park
Right: Water cascades off the tail of a diving humpback whale.

Bald Eagles

Southeast Alaska is the home to the largest bald eagle population in the nation. Approximately 15,000 bald eagles live in Southeast Alaska—more than in all of the other states combined. Biologist have counted 130 bald eagle nests from Berners Bay to Point Bishop. Native to North America and found nowhere else, these majestic birds of prey feed on fish and nest in the oldest trees at the edge of the old-growth forests, along saltwater shores.

Left: Bald eagle grabs a herring.
Above: Eagle in moonlight

Sea Lions

Just a half-hour by kayak from Eagle
Beach or ten minutes by skiff from
Almaga Harbor, Steller sea lions gather
on Benjamin Island. Although their
declining numbers throughout the rest of
the North Pacific have put them on the
endangered list, they continue to thrive at this
rookery. Much larger than seals, the females
weigh more than 500 pounds and the massive
bulls more than twice that much.

Left: Barking sea lion, Benjamin Island
Above: Sea lions at haul out, Benjamin Island

─ Benjamin Island Sea Lion Rookery ─

THE HEART OF TOWN

Anyone who lives here soon discovers that the weather is better "out the road." Maybe that's why the Tlingits chose Auke Bay, 13 miles north of downtown for their permanent winter village. But prospectors who staked the townsite picked the place closest to the gold. As the community grew, it spread out into flatlands left behind by the glaciers' retreat. Although more people now live in the Mendenhall Valley, downtown Juneau remains the community's gathering place. It is where we make our laws, march in parades and greet tourists. Vibrant neighborhoods still nestle at the base of Mount Juneau and Mount Roberts, which soar above the narrow city streets.

Left: An autumn view of one of Juneau's oldest neighborhoods, Starr Hill.
Above: Hawthorn tree in full bloom complements neighboring totem pole at Juneau-Douglas City Museum.

Celebration

Nurturing traditional native culture, Celebration grew from a 1980 gathering of elders. On their advice, Sealaska, the regional Native corporation, held the first Celebration in 1982. It comes back every two years. The multi-day event has grown to include 40 dance groups and more than 1,000 performers in regalia old and new. Traditional rhythms boom with overwhelming power in Juneau's Centennial Hall. Celebration is not only a colorful spectacle, but also a spiritual gathering, uniting people of common heritage and commitment.

Left: Proud Celebration 1996 participant
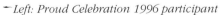
Right: Southeast Alaska Natives parade downtown.

"*The Western impact on the Tlingit people was such that the Native traditional singing and dancing and various ceremonials were put away. The Tlingit people, in appreciation of their traditions, felt they should bring them out again. You might call it a revival, a cultural renaissance.*"

DR. WALTER SOBOLEFF

— *Left: Dancer from Kake*
— *Above: Charlie Jimmie*
— *Right: Lillian Hillman*

~ CHILDREN'S CONCERT AT CELEBRATION '96 ~

"Since Celebration '82, we have seen cultural knowledge growing. For years, children were taught little or nothing of our traditions, but now many of them perform at Celebration—our children, our grandchildren and our great grandchildren. We are proud of them, and we entrust the safekeeping of our cultures to them."

DR. WALTER SOBOLEFF

Fourth of July

Juneau makes much of the Fourth of July. Like a big party, it spills out to gather up everybody in town, whether old-timers or tourists here just for the day. The tradition goes back decades to when the great gold mines were in full production and Independence Day was one of just two miners' holidays a year. The Fourth became a major community festival, with competitions pitting miners from the Alaska-Juneau Mine against those from the Treadwell Mine in Douglas. Douglas is now part of Juneau, but the rivalry continues with a full schedule of holiday events on both sides of the Gastineau Channel.

Above: Owen Kelley and competitor during Fourth of July sack races in Douglas.
Left: Fireworks display viewed from the shoulder of Mount Roberts.

—Fourth of July Downtown Juneau—

Small-town Soul

The event that epitomizes the prevailing small-town spirit is the Fourth of July parade. There are actually two of them. The parade in Douglas follows the one in Juneau, so those who quickly scurry across the bridge can be part of both. Along with the standard fare of decorated floats, the Douglas parade features dozens of costumed youngsters on decorated bikes. Juneau fields a marching band that plays and marches—and is working on doing both at the same time.

Lightening up Winter

With about 18 hours of darkness in mid-winter, we look for ways to brighten the long night. Christmas lights plugged in on Thanksgiving weekend are inclined to hang around until Valentine's Day. There is a spotlight on every stage, as the town turns out for live theater and musical performances. In between basketball games, every gym is home court to indoor soccer and volleyball. We head for the pool to swim a few laps and socialize in the sauna, or to the university's Marine Tech Center to mess around with boats. There are folkdances, barn dances, jitterbug classes, and black-tie, big-band nights. Juneauites are two-stepping and rockin' in the bars.

Above: Perseverance Theatre stage for the play "The Birds"

Left: Inside the Red Dog Saloon

Alaska Folk Festival

For the folk musicians and fans of their music, the Alaska Folk Festival is just as much a rite of spring as the lengthening daylight, unfurling skunk cabbage and emerging bears. Now in its third decade, the festival has evolved into a week of performances, workshops and informal jam sessions all over town. It brings life back to the street, where the April sun keeps fingers warm enough to play. It is a multi-generational event and every concert is free.

— Left: Three-year-old Scott Funk gets some pointers from a veteran player.

— Above: Workshop participant demonstrates an unconventional rhythm instrument made from a moose jawbone.

— Opposite page: Sun and laughter warm street musicians in downtown Juneau during an impromptu street jam.

Juneau • 1887

A Juneau Historical Scrapbook ·······································

A portrait of Juneau wouldn't be complete without a glimpse at its past. The community's collective memory unfolds a rich and colorful scrapbook of cultures and backgrounds, events and artifacts. Contemporary lifestyles and celebrations draw from this history—from the ancient Native tradition of reverence for the land, from the spunk and perseverance of gold prospectors and early white settlers, and from the dedication of generations who invested their lives in this town and called it home. The result is a spirit of immeasurable value; one that combines a sense of pride and tradition, a penchant for adventure and a willingness to look back and laugh.

NATIVE VILLAGE, JUNEAU • 1887

RICHARD HARRIS

KAWA.ÉE (KOWEE)

JOSEPH JUNEAU

8,000 B.C. NATIVE SETTLEMENT   **MID TO LATE 1700s** EUROPEAN EXPLORATION   **1867** U.S. PURCHASE   **1880** GOLD DISCOVERY

8,000 BC
● Native peoples settle along the coastline of what will become Southeast Alaska almost 10,000 years later.

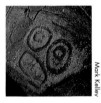

Mid-1700s
● Tlingit Indians and their complex and artistic culture thrive; the area boasts one of the largest human populations north of Mexico. In 1741 Russian explorer Alexei Chirikof records the first sighting of Alaska by a white man. He is followed by Spanish explorers in the mid-1770s and English adventurer Captain James Cook in 1778.

1794
● Explorer Captain George Vancouver names the island across Gastineau Channel from the mainland for Bishop John Douglas, who edited one of the accounts of Captain Cook's voyages. Douglas Island later thrived as a mining district and today offers a spectacular view of Juneau.

1867
● Secretary of State William Seward convinces the United States to purchase Alaska from Russia for $7.2 million. Thinking it a grand waste of money, newspapers dub the purchase *Seward's Folly* and *Seward's Ice Box.*

1879
● German mining engineer George Pilz of Sitka offers Indian leaders a reward of 100 Hudson's Bay blankets in exchange for identifying locations of gold-bearing ore. Kawa.ée (Kowee), a leader of the Auk Kwaan tribe piques Pilz's interest with samples of Gastineau Channel gold.

1880
● In July, Pilz sends down-and-out prospectors Joe Juneau and Richard Harris by canoe to explore Gastineau Channel. But it isn't until Kawa.ée personally leads the two men up Gold Creek to Silver Bow Basin that the prospectors become convinced they have found the mother lode. In October, Harris writes a code of local laws governing the "Harris Mining District" and stakes a 160-acre townsite along the Gastineau Channel beach, naming it Harrisburg. It is the first new town to be built in Alaska since the U.S. purchase. Three dozen or so Sitka prospectors spend a miserable winter in the new town, waiting for spring thaw to stake their claims.

1881
● In February, miners vote to change the name of Harrisburg to Rockwell, for Naval Lieutenant Commander Charles Rockwell. He is charged with arbitrating sometimes shaky relationships between miners and Auk and Taku Tlingits in the new settlement. Rockwell and his marines construct a military preserve and when they leave later in the year, turn over the buildings to the postmaster. As soon as Rockwell sails away, miners vote to change the town's name to Juneau

ASL: PCA 87/1887

MENDENHALL VALLEY

ASL: PCA 01/2144

CHINA JOE

ASL: PCA 312/80

ED WEBSTER ON TELEPHONE HILL

Alaska State Library PCA 01/1153

1895 *Front Street marks the high-tide line of the beach. Businesses to serve the growing mining population anchor the shore to the sea. Huge icebergs, torn from the face of the Taku Glacier south of town, drift into Gastineau Channel and must be towed away before the wind and tide dash the islands of ice into the docks and buildings clustered along the beach.*

1881 JUNEAU TOWN NAMED   **1883** FIRST TELEPHONE CO.   **1893** RUSSIAN ORTHODOX CHURCH BUILT

City. The postmaster drops the second part of the name.

● Sponsored by a group of San Francisco investors, former carpenter John Treadwell buys "French Pete" Erussard's claim on Douglas Island, just south of the present town of Douglas. Erussard's claim showed color but is a low-grade, hard-rock ore. Treadwell's enterprise opens a new era of mining in the Juneau area, transforming small placer efforts into underground operations that require sophisticated technical expertise and huge sums of capital.

● Navy Commander Glass reports Rockwell (earlier name of Juneau) has a population of 150 whites and 450 Indians.

1883

● Prospector Henry Roberts stakes claims on a mountain behind Juneau variously known as Bulgar Hill, Taku Hill, Mineral Hill and Jamestown Hill. The mountain is eventually named after the prospector and continues to be known today as Mount Roberts. A trail is carved out and a cross erected by community members in the early 1900s under the direction of Father Edward Brown.

● Ed Webster establishes the community's first telegraph company, which later becomes the telephone company. His home/business is built on the rock outcropping

downtown now called Telephone Hill. The rambling wood structure is still used as a residence but the state now owns the neighborhood — in case it decides to build a new capitol there.

● U.S. President Chester Arthur appoints John Kinkead as Alaska's first governor.

1886

● Racial prejudice inspires eviction of about 80 Chinese from Juneau. There is one notable exception: "China Joe" of Juneau, a bakery owner known to be generous with Juneau children and to share bread with gold miners when they are down on their luck.

1892

● The Auk Kwaan leader Kawa.ée dies at age 75.

1893

● The St. Nicholas Russian Orthodox Church is constructed, and in 1899, Holy Trinity Episcopal Church is built. Both continue to serve loyal congrega–tions today.

Mark Kelley

● Alaska Electric Light and Power Co. is started when Willis Thorpe sets up a generator and waterwheel on Gold Creek.

Treadwell Mine

Alaska State Library PCA 162/6

Early 1880s— early 1890s
The ban on importation of alcohol to Alaska doesn't prevent crafty saloon owners from inventing a system for stocking their shelves with beer and whiskey. When Seattle steamships arrive in the channel, the vessels' side doors open and crewmen shove wooden liquor barrels into the water that are "rescued" by barroom employees in skiffs.

Log Cabin Soda Works & City Brewery

Late 1880s—Early 1900s
Juneau simultaneously supports five breweries, even though city law says beer cannot be purchased unless it is accompanied by food. The thirsty buy a beer and sandwich, swilling the beer but returning the uneaten sandwich for a refund. The same stale grayish sandwich is shunted back and forth by patrons for days. Lord help those unfamiliar with the system who order lunch at a watering hole.

W.E. Nickell Collection

1900 POPULATION: 1,864   **1905** COURTHOUSE BUILT   **1906** GOVERNOR'S OFFICE IN JUNEAU   **1907** TONGASS NATIONAL FOREST CREATED

ASL: PCA 01/1218

1900
● The U.S. Census estimates Juneau's municipal population at 1,864.

● The Treadwell Mine Complex above Sandy Beach on Douglas Island pays the highest wages in the world: $2 daily for an Indian, $3 for a white man, $4 for a miner, $5 for a blacksmith and $6 for a millwright. At the height of production, the 960-stamp mill sets a world record, crushing 5,000 tons of ore daily. The rock crushers are loud, falling 96 times a minute.

● A Juneau family of five spends about $40 monthly on groceries. Milk is produced at the Calhoun Dairy not far from where the Federal Building is today. A pig farm — now the site of Juneau-Douglas High School — supplies residents with pork. The light company charges $1 monthly for every light bulb a household uses. Miners hunt grouse along the fringe of dark spruce above town, nick-naming the area Chicken Ridge.

1905
● A courthouse and jail is constructed (where the State Office Building now squats) and is so luxurious, men commit petty crimes at the start of autumn to be assured of a warm bed and full belly through the winter.

ASL: PCA 87/887

1906
● The governor's office is moved from Sitka to Juneau. Juneau residents have been battling to keep it here ever since. There have been seven full-fledged attempts to move the seat of government closer to Anchorage, but voters continue to defeat the effort.

1907
● The 17-million-acre Tongass National Forest — the largest national forest in the nation — is created by President Theodore Roosevelt.

1909
● In January, a 19-year-old pimp named Robert Franklin Stroud kills a bartender in downtown Juneau, after the saloon keeper injures Stroud's girlfriend. While serving his lifetime sentence for the murder — and two other prison stabbings — Stroud begins studying birds, eventually finding cures for several ornithological diseases. He is transferred to Alcatraz Island in San Francisco where he becomes known as "The Birdman of Alcatraz."

ALASKA TREADWELL MINE 1885-1904 • VALUE $21,817,296.19

Late 1880s— Early 1900s

With the largest and most efficient gold mines in the world, Juneau prospers. Alaska's first tramway, railroad and suspension bridge are built as infrastructure for the mines. Alaska's first bowling alley, tennis court, library, indoor swimming pool and opera house are built to amuse the miners. Three full shifts work around the clock; only on Christmas and the Fourth of July are the mines quiet. Death, as well as gold, is mined. Explosions, cave-ins and other accidents claim lives — as many as one a month during the life of the Treadwell.

MINERS

FIRST TERRITORIAL HOUSE OF REPRESENTATIVES • 1913

1912 ALASKA-GASTINEAU OPENS   **1913** WOMEN'S RIGHT TO VOTE   **1917** TREADWELL CAVE-IN   **1918** *PRINCESS SOPHIA* SINKS

1912

● Alaska is awarded territorial status and the Governor's Mansion is built.

● The Alaska Gastineau Mining Co. opens near Sheep Creek, in the now quiet neighborhood of Thane, three miles south of Juneau. At its peak in 1916, the Gastineau employs 940 men and crushes 12,000 tons of ore daily. The mine closes in 1921, a victim of its low-grade ore. In its brief nine-year life, however, the company produced $9.7 million in gold. Its workers set world records for high-volume, low-cost milling, and for such engineering feats as the largest dam, the longest tunnel and fastest tunneling.

1913

● The first law passed by the Alaska Territorial Legislature gives women the right to vote.

1916

● The Alaska-Juneau Mill is constructed at the base of Mount Roberts, south of Juneau. Tailings from the mine form the rock dump that extends into Gastineau Channel.

● The first Alaska statehood bill is introduced in the U.S. Congress.

1917

● A cave-in at the Treadwell Mine Complex south of present-day Douglas destroys all but one of the workings. Because the cave-in and flooding occur during a shift change, miraculously no one is killed. The ore finally runs out in 1922 and the mine is closed. At the height of production, the Treadwell employed 753 men and crushed 5,000 tons of ore daily, a world record at the time. The Treadwell was once the world's largest gold mining operation, producing $37 million in gold bullion. The town of Treadwell had a population of 522 in 1900, 1,222 in 1910 and 325 in 1920.

1918

● The steamship *Princess Sophia* runs aground at Vanderbilt Reef during a terrible storm. The ship's captain, believing the seas too turbulent for a safe rescue and convinced his vessel is still sound, rejects attempts to remove his passengers. During the night, the boat is pounded into bits and all 343 people aboard drown.

LAST TRACE OF THE PRINCESS SOPHIA

PURPLE FLASHES • 1926

SOUTH FRANKLIN ST. LANDSLIDE

CAPITOL BUILDING • 1931

For Good Light at Low cost

MAZDA

GE

EDISON MAZDA LAMPS

ALASKA ELECTRIC LIGHT & POWER CO.

JUNEAU - Phone 6   DOUGLAS - Phone 18

1923 PRESIDENT HARDING VISITS   **1928** KIMBALL PIPE ORGAN   **1931** FEDERAL BUILDING   **1933** SHRINE OF ST. THERESE

1920
- Disastrous landslide roars down Mt. Roberts, stopping at South Franklin. Three are killed, many are injured and six buildings are destroyed.

1923
- President Warren Harding visits Juneau.

1926
- Fire breaks out in the Native village near Douglas, leaving 42 Indian families homeless. The blaze spreads to the shutdown Treadwell buildings and to Douglas, where 38 homes are destroyed. It is a devastating blow for a community waiting for Treadwell to reopen.

- Elks' musical comedy presents the American Rocket Dancers as the *Purple Flashes*.

1928
- The Kimball Pipe Organ is installed in the Coliseum Theater by businessman W.D. Gross. In 1970, the organ is purchased by a Juneau family and given to the state in 1975. The refurbished organ is installed in the State Office Building in 1977. Today, free organ concerts frequently are given at noon Fridays.

- The Juneau High School Building is dedicated. Presently it is Capital Elementary School.

1931
- Juneau's original federal building is constructed for territorial offices. The block-wide brick building later is converted into the state's Capitol.

1933
- Volunteers begin construction on the log retreat house at the Shrine of St. Therese. The stone chapel is started in 1937. The first service is held there on October 26, 1941.

1934
- An English bull terrier named Patsy Ann is appointed "Official Greeter of Juneau" by the mayor. Despite being both deaf and mute, Patsy Ann meets every incoming ship at the dock, day or night. When Patsy

Ann dies in 1942, her coffin is lowered over the dock while a grieving crowd looks on. In 1992, a bronze statue of Patsy Ann is presented to the community by a citizens group. The sculpture sits on the dock facing the mouth of the channel, just as the real dog did, to welcome all who arrive by sea.

RUINS OF THE DOUGLAS FIRE

SHRINE OF SAINT THERESE

SALMON DERBY CONTESTANT

1935 FIRST DOUGLAS BRIDGE   **1937** DOUGLAS FIRE   **1938** FIRST SEATTLE AIR MAIL   **1938** FIRST GOLDEN NORTH SALMON DERBY

1935

● The second radio station in Alaska begins broadcasting in Juneau. KINY later adds television equipment, but because TV programs from the Lower 48 must be shipped to Alaska, residents become accustomed to watching national news broadcasts and important events a day late and Christmas specials aired long after New Year's. KINY is still a popular radio station in the Capital City, which in 1996 has five radio stations, a commercial TV station, a public TV station and more than four dozen cable TV channels to choose from.

● The Douglas Bridge is built to connect the island with the mainland. The cost: $255,000.

1936

● Mary Joyce, *Miss Juneau 1936,* enters the Miss Alaska competition by mushing a dog team more than 1,000 miles to Fairbanks in the dead of winter. She doesn't win the beauty contest but Fairbanks residents are so impressed, they make her an honorary member of the Pioneer Women of Alaska.

● A mud slide off Mt. Roberts kills 14 before stopping at Franklin Street.

1937

● Another disastrous fire in Douglas, fanned by high winter winds, consumes whole blocks of the town, including 20 businesses and 20 homes, leaving a large part of the community without shelter. The school, churches, city offices, fire hall and social halls are all lost.

1938

● The first air mail flight from Seattle dazzles Juneau residents who gather at the tiny airfield building to greet the plane with speeches and a brass band. That fall, the first Flying Boat — a Pan American Clipper — arrives in Auke Bay. A ticket to Seattle costs $95 and the flight lasts seven hours. Today a one-way ticket costs close to $400 and takes a little over two hours.

● Juneau establishes the Golden North Salmon Derby — for many the fishing highlight of the summer. Hundreds of prizes are given out and proceeds from the derby are awarded as youth scholarships.

GOLDEN NORTH SALMON DERBY JULY 19-20-21 1957 JUNEAU "GOIN' FISHIN'"

ALASKA-JUNEAU MILL

WAR NURSES • 1943

ASL: PCA 87/972

1939 BARANOF HOTEL OPENS   **1942** *USS JUNEAU* SINKS   **1944** ALASKA-JUNEAU MINE CLOSES   **1945** RACIAL DISCRIMINATION BANNED

1939

● The first commercial radio-telephone service is established between Juneau and Seattle.

● The Baranof Hotel is formally opened.

1941-45

● Juneau bustles with activity as a military port of call. The *USS Juneau* is sunk in the Battle of Guadalcanal on November 13, 1942. Aboard the ship are the five Sullivan brothers. The tragedy of one family losing so many of their children at one time prompts the U.S. Defense Department to change the way it assigns wartime duties. In 1987, the newest navy version of the *USS Juneau* sails into

town and survivors of the 1942 sinking are honored during Fourth of July festivities.

● President Franklin Roosevelt tries, unsuccessfully, to catch a salmon off Aaron Island as he stops off, secretly, on his way back from an inspection on the Aleutian Islands.

1944

● Juneau's last operating gold mine, the Alaska-Juneau above the rock dump, closes due to high costs and the manpower shortages of World War II. In the late 1930s, during peak production years, over 1,000 men worked three daily shifts. The A-J produced $80.8 million in gold (at $20 to $35 an ounce). The closure of

the A-J ended 64 years of mining and milling in the Juneau and Douglas area. The three mining giants extracted $158 million in gold, making Juneau the hard-rock mining capital of the world.

1945

● The Alaska Territorial Legislature votes to ban racial discrimina-tion, follow-ing a stirring speech given to lawmakers by a 34-year-old

ELIZABETH PERATROVICH

ASL: PCA 01/3294

Tlingit woman named Elizabeth Peratrovich. "I would not have expected that I, who am barely out of savagery, would have to remind gentlemen with 5,000 years of recorded civilization behind them of our Bill of Rights," she began. When she finished, there were tears and wild cheers.

1946

● A Juneau delegation hosts five-star General Omar Bradley on a local sportfishing expedition. The commit-tee arranges for fishing gear, transpor-tation and provisions but forgets to buy the famous general a non-resident fishing license. The general and local dignitaries are happily fishing when a federal wildlife agent

Alaska's Flag

GOLD MEDAL CHAMPIONS

GOVERNOR WILLIAM EGAN

1947 FIRST GOLD MEDAL BASKETBALL TOURNAMENT   **1950** POPULATION: 5,956   **1953** FIRST PLYWOOD MILL   **1959** ALASKA STATEHOOD

comes upon them, arresting Bradley and confiscating his gear. Later, after the general promises "never to do it again," the charges are dropped and the gear is returned.

1947

● The first Gold Medal Basketball Tournament is held in Juneau. Teams from virtually every town and village in Southeast now compete annually, and hundreds of their family members, friends and supporters fill the town.

● The elegant Waldorf Astoria in New York City serves ice imported from Juneau's Mendenhall Glacier to cool the cocktails at a prestigious publisher's party.

1949

● The 17th Coast Guard District is established.

1950

● U.S. Census takers estimate Juneau's population at 5,956.

● Eugene La Moore is hung on April 14 after he murders a Juneau grocer during a robbery. He is the last Juneau resident executed for a crime. Capital punishment is repealed in 1957.

1953

● A plywood mill is established in Juneau.

1956

● Higher education arrives in Juneau when a college is established in the old public school building near Capital School. The cornerstone is laid for the new $2 million Juneau-Douglas High School.

1958

● Congress passes the Alaska Statehood Act by a 208-166 vote in the U.S. House and a 64-20 vote in the Senate. Alaska newspaper headlines scream: "We're In!" An enormous celebration includes a parade downtown led by Benny Benson, an Alaska Native who designed the Big Dipper state flag. He was 13 when he won the flag design contest in 1926.

1959

● On January 3, President Dwight Eisenhower proclaims Alaska the 49th state.

● William Egan is the first governor elected by popular vote in Alaska. Famous for his photographic memory, an invaluable talent for a politician, Egan remembers people's names and everything about them, years after they are introduced. During his term, it's discovered his young son has built an amateur brewery in the basement of the Governor's Mansion. That mischievous boy — Dennis Egan — later is elected Juneau's mayor.

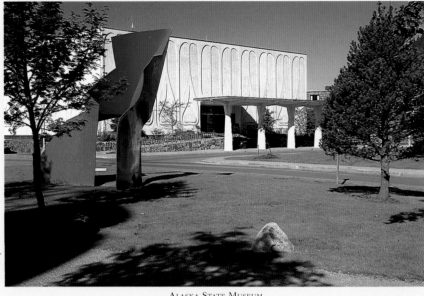

ALASKA STATE MUSEUM

SNETTISHAM HYDROELECTRIC PROJECT

1960 ALASKA MARINE HIGHWAY   **1965** AJ MILL FIRE   **1967** SNETTISHAM HYDRO PROJECT BEGUN   **1967** ALASKA CENTENNIAL

1960

● The U.S. Census Bureau estimates Juneau's population at 9,745.

● Voters approve bonds for the creation of the Alaska Marine Highway System to ferry passengers from Washington State to Alaska. In 1996, the system comprises eight large vessels traveling to 32 ports of call.

1962

● The Mendenhall Glacier Visitor's Center opens.

1964

● The federal government lists the Juneau Airport as the "un-busiest" of all FAA-controlled airports in the nation. The airport is renovated in 1987 and now serves thousands of

residents and visitors. In 1995, almost 390,000 commercial air passengers fly through the airport.

1965

● The Federal Building is constructed on land once used by locals as a baseball diamond.

● Juneau's most visible landmark, the old Alaska-Juneau Mill just south of town, burns to the ground.

1967

● The contract for the $50 million federal Snettisham hydroelectric project is signed. When it is completed, the price tag turns out to be $170 million. Juneau continues to get its power from this plant, located about 38 air miles south of town.

● Alaska's Centennial is celebrated, commemorating the day the region changed ownership from Russia to the United States.

1968

● The Alaska State Museum is built, paid for by a sales tax approved by Juneau voters.

1970

● The U.S. Census pegs Juneau's population at 13,556.

● Voters agree to unify into one municipality, the City and Borough of Juneau. When the ballots are counted, 71 percent of the residents of the City of Douglas have voted against unification. The Alaska Supreme Court eventually dismisses a community

lawsuit that would have allowed Douglas to remain independent.

● The Sierra Club and the Alaska Conservation Society file for a court injunction to prevent construction of a $100 million pulp mill-sawmill complex at Berners Bay, 40 miles north of downtown Juneau.

1971

● On September 4, an Alaska Airlines jet crashes on its approach to Juneau, killing all 111 people aboard, the worst aviation disaster at that time in America. The Boeing 727 jet smashes into the 2,500-foot level of a 3,500-foot mountain 21 miles west of Juneau. It takes a week to recover the bodies.

THIRTEENTH ANNUAL
ALASKA FOLK FESTIVAL
CENTENNIAL HALL · APRIL 6-12

Bill Hudson

"Women with Hair" at the Alaska Folk Festival

Mark Kelley

Mark Kelley

Dipac Hatchery

Eaglecrest Ski Area

Mark Kelley

1971 ANCSA SIGNED   **1973** PIPELINE CONSTRUCTION BEGINS   **1975** FIRST ALASKA FOLK FESTIVAL   **1976** DIPAC HATCHERY

● Congress approves the Alaska Native Claims Settlement Act (ANCSA), granting Alaska Natives title to 40 million acres and $962.5 million. The Juneau-based Sealaska Corporation is one of the 13 regional corporations created by the act. The Settlement Act is needed for construction of the oil pipeline.

● The 67-bed Bartlett Memorial Hospital opens near Salmon Creek, three miles north of downtown Juneau.

1972

● Following a record snowfall, an avalanche in the Last Chance Basin knocks out the city's water supply for five days.

1973

● The trans-Alaska oil pipeline receives final approval and in 1974 construction begins on the haul road to move supplies to Prudhoe Bay.

1975

● The first Alaska Folk Festival is held in Juneau — a one-night concert of local musicians who perform on a small stage in the Alaska State Museum. The festival is now a week-long extravaganza of evening and weekend concerts featuring new performers every 15 minutes. The concerts and more than 30 work-shops attract "folkies" from through-out the Pacific Northwest.

1976

● Juneau's private nonprofit salmon hatchery, Douglas Island Pink and Chum (DIPAC), begins replenishing area waters with fish. Originally there are dozens of canneries and process-ing facilities in and around Juneau, and there are so many fish in Salmon Creek it is difficult to wade across the stream. But fish begin to disappear and Juneau fishermen are forced to harvest catches farther and farther from home.

● When Juneau's last two processing plants burn down, it is thought the local commercial fishing industry has gone up in smoke. In 1984, however, marine biologist Sandro Lane begins using an old family recipe to

alchemize salmon into lox in the garage of his Mendenhall Valley home. Taku Smokeries has expanded several times since, and provides employment for both cold storage workers and fishermen.

TAKU SMOKERIES
JUNEAU ALASKA

● The municipally owned Eaglecrest Ski Area opens, covering 640 acres on Douglas Island. It features 30-some trails, two chair lifts and a 1,400 foot vertical drop.

91

Mark Kelley

Nimbus

Jere Smith

85
NIMBUS IN LIMBO

PERSEVERANCE
T·H·E·A·T·R·E

PURE GOLD

An oral drama of
Juneau's past told
by six people who
lived it. PURE GOLD
will be presented by
Perseverance Theatre
In Douglas on Third St., 8:15 P.M.
June 1 - Sept. 1, Monday - Friday
Tickets available through
Baranof Book Store
Call 364-2421 for reservations

Bill C. Ray

UNIVERSITY OF ALASKA SOUTHEAST

1977 *NIMBUS* SCULPTURE INSTALLED   **1979** PERSEVERANCE THEATRE FOUNDED   **1980** ALASKA PERMANENT FUND ESTABLISHED   **1980** ALASKA TIME

1977

● *Nimbus*, the outdoor sculpture Juneau loves to hate, is designed by New York artist Robert Murray and installed in 1978 next to the Dimond Courthouse downtown. The first piece of abstract artwork ever publicly commissioned in Alaska, *Nimbus* is a lightning rod for controversy, the butt of many jokes, and the center of heated debate on the value and definition of public art. In 1984, *Nimbus* becomes the first piece of public art in the nation to be removed and dumped in the mud at a state storage yard. In 1990, a group of *Nimbus* supporters raise private money to erect the displaced sculpture on the lawn of the Alaska State Museum.

● The first oil flows through the trans-Alaska pipeline.

1979

● Perseverance Theatre in Douglas is founded and presents its first production, *Pure Gold*, an original play drawn from stories of early Juneau. The professional theater company is now the largest in the state and has earned an international reputation for innovation and creativity.

● Two Juneau police officers are shot and killed and another badly injured downtown by a deranged mail clerk waiting in ambush. The tragic episode closes when the mail clerk commits suicide. One of Juneau's most popular recreation areas, Adair-

Kennedy Memorial Park, is named after the two deceased men.

1980

● The U.S. Census estimates Juneau's population at 19,528.

● The Juneau Douglas Community College downtown and Southeast Senior College in Auke Bay are merged to become the University of Alaska Juneau. In 1987, the university system is reorganized and the college is renamed the University of Alaska Southeast. Enrollment in 1996 includes more than 600 full-time students and 2,000 part-time students.

● The Legislature repeals the state income tax and establishes the Alaska Permanent Fund.

● A fight breaks out over a proposal to reduce Alaska's five time zones to two. Eventually the Capital City, and most of the rest of the state, is placed in a new time zone called Alaska Time.

JUNEAU-DOUGLAS BRIDGES

CENTENNIAL HALL

1980 JUNEAU CENTENNIAL   **1981** 2ND JUNEAU-DOUGLAS BRIDGE   **1983** CENTENNIAL HALL OPENS   **1984** THANKSGIVING DAY STORM

● Fire erupts on the cruise ship *Prinsendam* in the Gulf of Alaska and 529 people are evacuated to Juneau. The ship sinks.

● Juneau celebrates its centennial with a six-ton, 34-foot-long birthday cake. Mickey Mouse leads the Fourth of July parade.

1981

● State Senator George Hohman of Bethel is convicted of bribery by a Juneau Superior Court jury. He is later sentenced to prison and becomes the first Alaska senator tossed out of office.

● Republican-led lawmakers stage a surprise coup in the state House, ousting Juneau Democratic Representative Jim Duncan as House speaker.

● The second Juneau-Douglas bridge replaces the first one. The modern bridge costs $25.1 million. For a short time, both bridges span Gastineau Channel.

1982

● Voters reject a $2.8 billion bond issue to pay for moving the capital to Willow. Opponents hand out sponges to illustrate the fiscal impact of the $3 billion price tag. The bond issue arose from a successful 1974 initiative to move the capital to Southcentral Alaska.

● Celebration '82, a gathering of some of Southeast Alaska's best Native dance troupes, attracts hundreds of participants to Juneau. Held every other year in early summer, the cultural event is a celebration of Alaska Native traditions and ceremonies.

● McDonald's opens in the Mendenhall Valley. Juneau comes of age in the fast-food generation when the hamburger restaurant arrives.

1983

● Juneau's Centennial Hall and a new elementary school near the Mendenhall River are constructed. Fed by oil dollars, Juneau's economy booms.

1984

● The Thanksgiving Day storm, which combines high tides and even higher winds, causes widespread destruction to waterfront property.

● A disgruntled former employee sets fire to the newly renovated Baranof Hotel. No one is killed, but a 15-foot fireball explodes from the front door of the downtown hotel. Damages are estimated at $1.5 million.

Mark Kelley/Juneau Empire

JOE GORILLA AND BELLE BLUE

photo: Mark Kelley   handlining: S. Kraft

NAA KAHIDI THEATER

GOEFF AND MARCIE LARSON

1984 PARKING GARAGE CONTROVERSY　　**1985-86** ECONOMY NOSEDIVES　　**1986** JUNEAU JUMPERS ORGANIZED　　**1986** NAA KAHIDI THEATER FOUNDED

1984

● Belle Blue, an eccentric citizen advocate known for dressing in Klondike-era costumes, challenges the city's plans to construct a parking garage on the waterfront. Municipal officials fail to take her seriously until she wins a court injunction halting the project. She acts as her own attorney and manages to take the case all the way to the Alaska Supreme Court. The city eventually wins, and the parking garage is built. Architectural awards are won for the library later built as an afterthought atop the concrete structure.

1985

● Write-in candidate Joe Gorilla (aka Jeff Brown) runs for mayor against Belle Blue, Peggie Garrison and Ernie Polley. Joe Gorilla pledges to eliminate sales tax on bananas. Polley wins.

● Juneau begins to feel the downside of its building boom as oil prices tumble.

GOD, Please give us another Boom -we promise not to piss this one away!

● Bill Sheffield, rocked by a scandal involving alleged improper bidding practices on a state project, is the first Alaska governor to weather impeachment hearings. The Alaska Senate fails to impeach him, but he loses the next gubernatorial primary.

1986

● The Juneau Jumpers, a precision jump-roping group, organizes. Con–sidered the best of its kind in the world now, the team wins gold medals in national and international competi-tions, performing around the globe.

● Juneau's economy nosedives as oil prices plummet, resulting in layoffs, a stagnant real estate market,

bankrupt businesses and slashed government budgets.

● Naa Kahidi Theater is founded, presenting dramas based on Native legends and history throughout the U.S., Canada and Europe.

● Marcie and Goeff Larson, a young couple interested in homebrewing as a hobby, establish the Alaskan Brewing and Bottling Co. One of contemporary Juneau's shining success stories, the brewery expands its production every few years. The beer it produces at its Lemon Creek plant wins gold medals at the most prestigious national and international brewing competitions.

Mark Kelley/Juneau Empire

GOVERNOR STEVE COWPER

Mark Kelley/Juneau Empire

JUNEAU COLD STORAGE FIRE

PACKED BY
COLD STORAGE
COMPANY INC.
356 SOUTH FRANKLIN
JUNEAU, ALASKA 99801
JUNEAU ALASKA SEA FOODS

JUNEAU IS JUST FINE WITHOUT THE AJ MINE

Import Miners
Export Whiners

Mark Kelley

AJ MINE ADIT

1987 JUNEAU COLD STORAGE FIRE   **1987** FIRST CAPITAL SCHOOL CLOSURE   **1988** JOHN KENNETH PEEL TRIAL   **1989** NAVY HOMEPORT DEFEATED

● A Juneau man steals his neighbor's car, burglarizes a liquor store, steals booze and bags of snack food. He returns the neighbor's car damaged and police follow a Hansel and Gretel trail of *Cheetos* to the thief's front door. The press identifies the hapless burglar as the *Cheeto Bandito.*

● In May, Juneau prepares for a tsunami, following an Aleutian Island earthquake measuring 7.7 on the Richter Scale. The tsunami waves turns out to be only about 2 inches high and residents plaster bumper stickers on their cars reading "I Survived the Tsunami of 1986."

1987
● With borrowed hat, rifle and horse, newly elected Governor Steve Cowper poses as the "High Plains Drifter." He earned the title of the Clint Eastwood movie character as the strong, silent-type leader of the House Finance Committee in 1976-77.

● Capital School closes, despite protests from downtown parents. It later reopens, only to face another closure in 1997.

● The abandoned Juneau Cold Storage burns down; it takes firefighters 40 hours to battle the blaze.

● Black bears in record numbers wander the streets and backyards of downtown residents, pawing through

Dumpsters and garbage cans. Some 15 bruins are killed by law enforcement authorities. Following protests by outraged residents, officials experiment with other tactics to discourage black bears from acquiring a fatal taste for garbage.

1988
● Between July 1 and November 30, rain falls on all but 19 days.

● The longest and most expensive criminal trial in Alaska history concludes when a Juneau Superior Court jury acquits John Kenneth Peel, a 27-year-old Washington State

fisherman, of eight counts of murder and one count of arson.

1989
● In February 1989, a devastating cold snap locks up the entire state. Juneau shivers but enjoys the lengthiest stretch of blue skies since 1881.

● Voters turn down a proposal to encourage the U.S. Navy to build a homeport in Juneau.

● Fiery debate erupts when a Canadian corporation announces plans to re-open the Alaska-Juneau mine three miles from the heart of downtown.

Mark Kelley/Juneau Empire

FORMER PRESIDENT GERALD FORD AT THE MENDENHALL GOLF COURSE

Mark Kelley

HILARY LINDH

GREENS CREEK MINE WORKERS

POT GOT MORE VOTES THAN HICKEL.

1989 *EXXON VALDEZ* OIL SPILL   **1989** GREENS CREEK MINE OPENS   **1992** LINDH WINS OLYMPIC MEDAL   **1993** POPULATION: 28,791

1989

● On March 24, the *Exxon Valdez* supertanker goes aground on Bligh Reef in Prince William Sound, spilling an unprecedented 11.3 million gallons of crude oil. Virtually overnight, the spill creates "spillionaires," people who make enormous sums of money from cleanup efforts, and "oil spill widow(er)s," the spouses of government and private industry workers sent "to the front for the duration."

● Greens Creek Mine on Admiralty Island opens up. It is the largest underground silver producer in North America.

1990

● The U.S. Census counts 26,751 residents in Juneau.

● Walter J. Hickel, a former Republican governor and a third-party candidate, is elected governor with 39 percent of the popular vote. He jumps into the election at the last minute, under the banner of the Alaskan Independence Party, and wins after seven weeks of campaigning.

In the same election, Alaskans vote to recriminalize the private possession of marijuana, striking down the country's most liberal pot law. The measure passes, 54 percent for and 46 percent against. A bumper sticker points out the political oddity that more people voted to keep marijuana legal than voted for Hickel as governor.

● Former U.S. President Gerald Ford drops by Juneau on his vacation to play golf at the nine-hole Mendenhall Golf Course.

1991

● A mildewed Juneau sets a new annual record for rain — 85.15 inches of precipitation. The previous record, set in 1961, is 68.11 inches.

● An Oregon serial killer ends his homicide spree in Juneau when he murders a 39-year-old Greens Creek miner. John Fauntenberry is arrested and confesses to five other killings.

1992

● Juneau's Hilary Lindh wins the Olympic silver medal for downhill skiing in Meribel, France. It is the first individual Olympic medal ever awarded an Alaskan.

● On November 12, an Alaska Army National Guard twin-engine aircraft, flying to the Capital City from Anchorage, crashes outside of Juneau, killing all eight aboard. The dead include the brigadier general commanding the National Guard and the Guard's highest ranking enlisted man, Sergeant Major Archie Kahklen of Juneau.

THIGH-DEEP SNOW AT EAGLECREST

Mark Kelley

BISHOP MICHAEL KENNY

Mark Kelley

MOUNT ROBERTS TRAM

1994 RECORD SNOWFALL   **1994** ULMER ELECTED, FIRST FEMALE LIEUTENANT GOVERNOR   **1994** CAPITAL MOVE DEFEATED   **1996** MOUNT ROBERTS TRAM OPENS

1993

● The municipal government estimates Juneau's population at 28,791.

● It is the warmest year on record for Juneau: the average daily temperature is 44.2 degrees. The hottest day of the year is in July: 79 degrees. The highest temperature ever recorded in Juneau is 90 degrees in July 1975. (The coldest is minus 22 degrees, set in February 1968 and January 1972.)

1994

● Juneau survives the snowiest year on record — 212 inches — 69.8 inches of which falls in November.

● Fran Ulmer, Juneau's former mayor, becomes the first female lieutenant governor in Alaska.

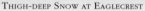

● After a strident campaign, Alaskans defeat an initiative to move the capital to Wasilla. They do approve the FRANK initiative, which requires voter approval of bonding for a new capital.

● Hilary Lindh wins the World Cup downhill race in Sierra Nevada, Spain, and competes with the U.S. Ski team in the winter Olympics in Lillehammer, Norway.

● Juneau's new middle school is named Dzantik'i Heeni, Tlingit for "where the flounders gather."

1995

● The beloved 57-year-old Catholic Bishop Michael Kenny — known affectionately as "The Bish" — dies suddenly of a brain aneurysm while visiting Jordan in February. More than 1,600 people attend his funeral and later the burial at the Shrine of St. Therese.

● The newly established Mount Roberts Development Corporation wins a permit to construct a tramway from the waterfront to the 1,800-foot level of Mount Roberts. The following year, the tram opens.

● The Juneau-Douglas High School Drill Team wins three first places in national competition held in Los Angeles. It is the first time any team has won the Triple Crown. The team goes on to win the world championship in Japan.

● The municipality estimates Juneau's population at 29,755.

97

MARK KELLEY

Juneau Portrait II is Mark Kelley's fourth book of photos. In 1995, Epicenter Press released Mark's *Alaska's Ocean Highways: A Travel Adventure Aboard Northern Ferries.* Fairweather Press has published two books featuring his black and white photography: *Juneau Portrait* in 1982 and *Heartbeat: World Eskimo Indian Olympics* in 1986. Mark also publishes a line of notecards called Coho Photo Notes, and calendars of both Juneau and Southeast Alaska.

Mark has been a freelance photographer for the past 20 years. His photos have been featured on the covers of more than 50 publications including Alaska and national magazines, books, brochures, calendars and annual reports.

Born and raised in Buffalo, NY, Mark moved to Alaska in 1974. He attended the University of Alaska Fairbanks and graduated in 1978 with a degree in journalism and northern studies. He worked as the *Juneau Empire*'s photographer for 14 years until he left in 1993 to freelance full-time.

Mark lives in Juneau with his wife, Jan Beauchamp, and two sons, Gabe and Owen.

ANNABEL LUND

Annabel Lund has lived in Alaska since 1975 and in Juneau since 1981. A reporter, editor and news director in newspapers, radio and television, she has authored three books. This is her second collaboration with Mark Kelley.

In July 1996, she took a year's leave of absence from Juneau to perform relief work in Bosnia. Her heart, however, remains here, in the mountains, seas and skies of home.